Clara Schumann's Piano Notebook

by Gail Smith

© 2020 BY MEL BAY PUBLICATIONS, INC.
ALL RIGHTS RESERVED. MADE AND PRINTED IN U.S.A.
No part of this publication may be reproduced in whole or in part, or stored in a retrieval system, or transmitted in any form
or by any means, electronic, mechanical, photocopy, recording, or otherwise, without written permission of the publisher.

Visit us at www.melbay.com — E-mail us at email@melbay.com

Table of Contents

Polonaise in E♭ major, Op. 1, No. 1 4

Prelude, Op. 16, No. 2 7

Romance, Op. 21, No. 2 10

Mazurka, Op. 6, No. 3 14

Scherzo, Op. 14 18

Nocturne, Op. 6, No. 2 28

Romance, Op. 3 34
    Introduction 34
    Theme "Romanza" 34
    Variation 1 35
    Variation 2 37
    Variation 3 38
    Variation 4 39
    Variation 5 41
    Variation 6 42
    Variation 7 44
    Variation 8 46

CLARA SCHUMANN

Clara was born on September 13, 1819 in Leipzig, Germany. Her parents were Marianne and Frederick Wieck. Marianne was a former piano student of Frederick, however, as his wife she was under a great deal of pressure from him to practice, teach and perform. When Clara was five, her mother left and divorced her controlling husband. Clara and her two younger brothers had to stay with their father as German law required. Clara didn't talk until she was five years old when her father began giving her piano lessons with two other little girls. Soon her father realized she had talent and wasn't deaf or delayed as had been thought.

Clara began having an hour piano lesson with her father every day and was required to practice for two more hours. She enjoyed playing the piano and pleasing her father. Frederick was amazed at her ability to memorize a short piece after hearing it once. He decided that he could turn Clara into a piano virtuoso and become the most famous piano teacher in Germany.

When Clara was eleven her father began taking her on concert tours where she performed her own compositions along with pieces by Bach, Beethoven, and Mendelssohn. She was the first to play the music of Chopin.

Clara's outstanding piano performances brought many new students to her father. Robert Schumann was so impressed with Clara's ability, he began piano lessons with her father, Robert was nine years older than Clara and said that she played the piano far better than he did. Clara even composed a concerto when only thirteen that Robert helped her orchestrate. Mendelssohn conducted the premier performance when she was sixteen.

Long story short, as time went on, Robert and Clara fell in love. When her father realized they were in love, he became extremely angry. He told her she could never speak to Robert or have any contact with him again. In a rage, Frederick told Clara that he would shoot Robert if she ever saw him again.

Frederick planned a long concert tour to keep her away from Robert. Clara gave concerts in Vienna and she became so famous that the restaurants there made a dessert named after her, "Torte a la Wieck." Clara played so fantastic that the Austrian emperor conferred the title, "Royal and Imperial Chamber Virtuoso" to her.

Several years later after heartache, tension, turmoil and sorrow, the lovers went to court and finally were allowed to marry when she was twenty-one. They married the day before her birthday with only her mother and minister there.

A new chapter began for Clara. She was busy teaching and giving concerts and her husband would compose music all the time. They had eight children, one died when a year old. Clara continued giving concerts in England, Paris, Russia, Germany and many other countries. She played Robert's piano compositions in all her concerts. He had injured his hand and was not able to concertize.

As time went on, Robert showed signs of mental illness and when Clara was thirty-four years old and seven months pregnant, Robert jumped off a bridge into the Rhine. Fortunately, he was rescued by fishermen that had seen what happened. He was brought to a mental hospital and died two years later.

Clara continued giving concerts to support her children. She had incredible stamina and lived to be seventy-six. Clara said, "It is a beautiful thing to be able to put your feelings into sound."

Polonaise in E♭ major, Op. 1, No. 1

Clara Schumann
Op. 1, No. 1

Prelude, Op. 16, No. 2

Clara Schumann
Op. 16, No. 2

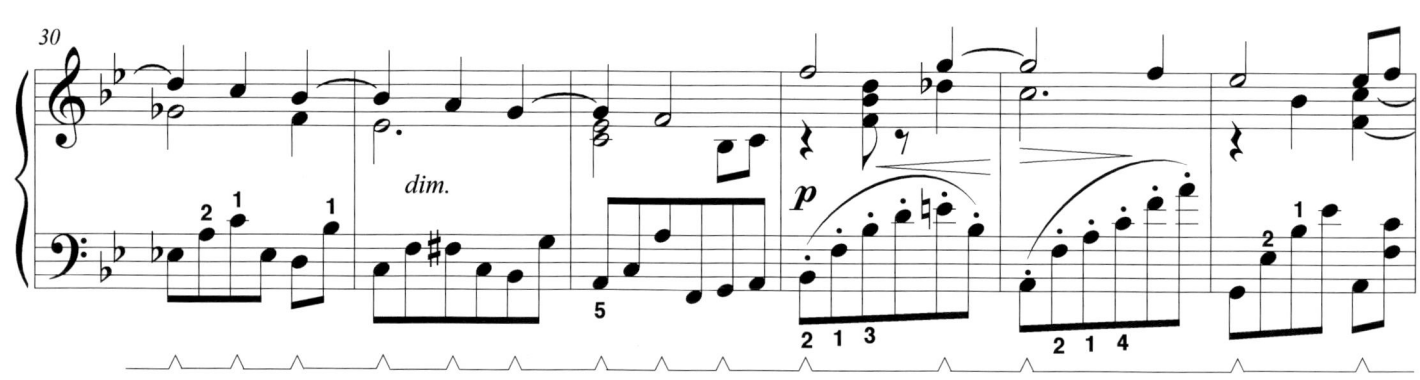

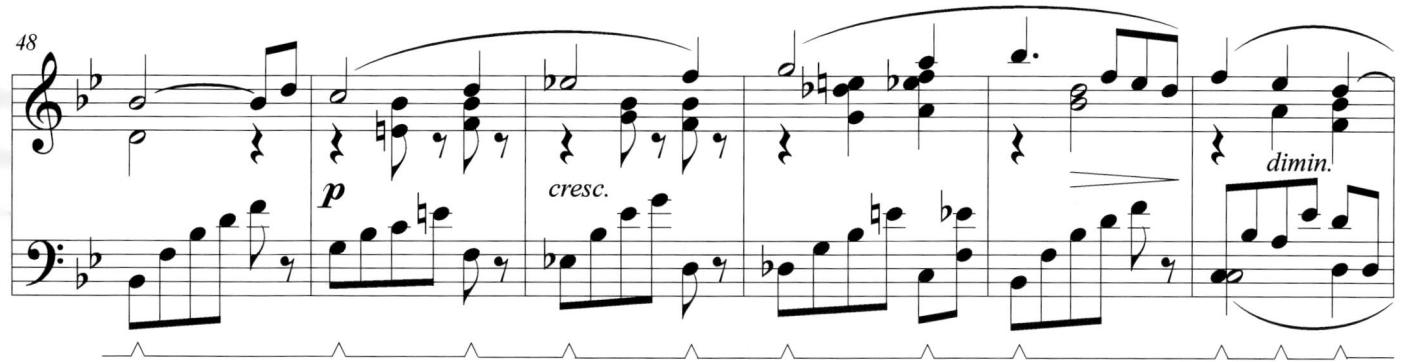

Romance, Op. 21, No. 2

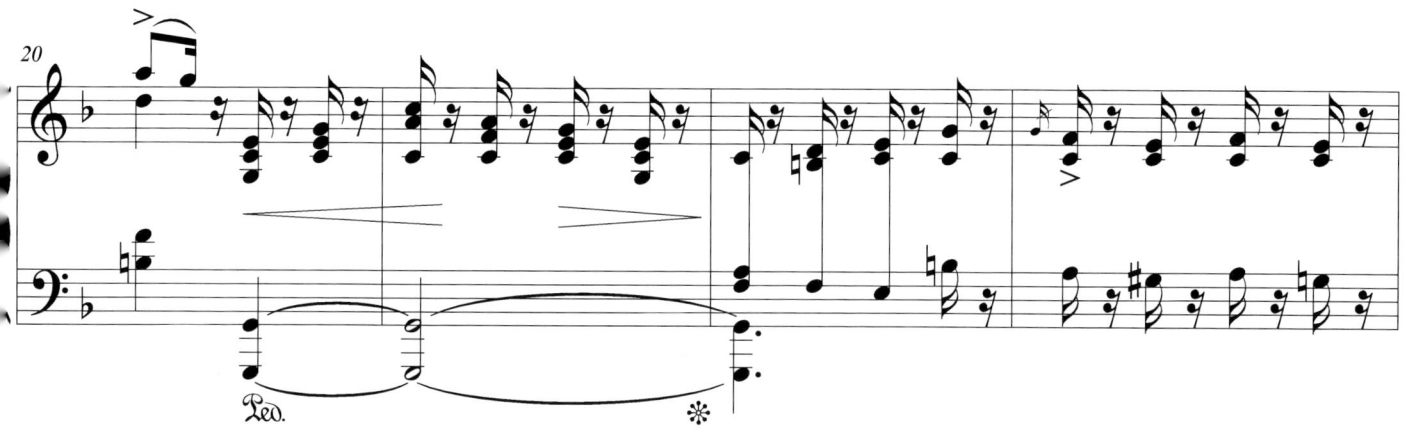

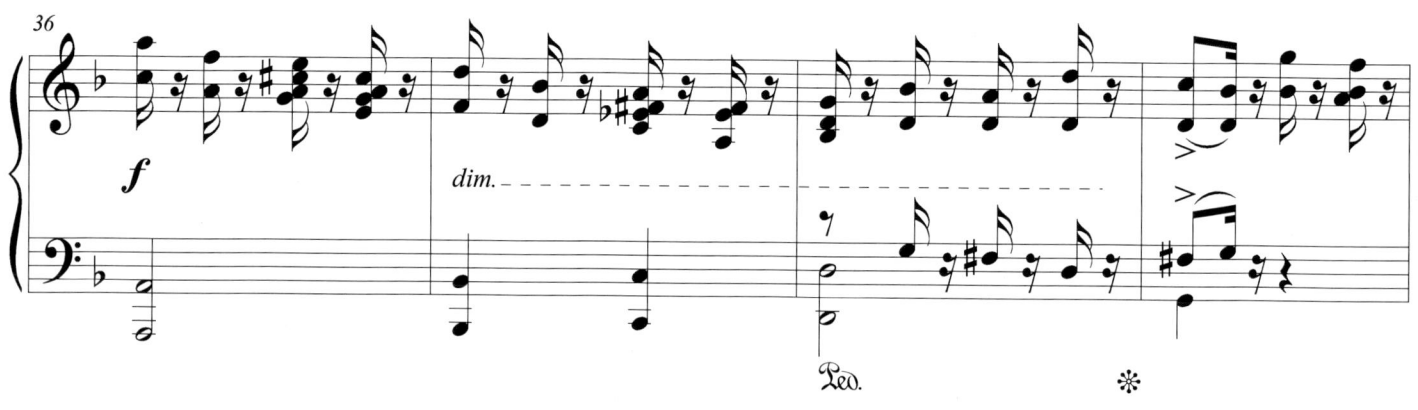

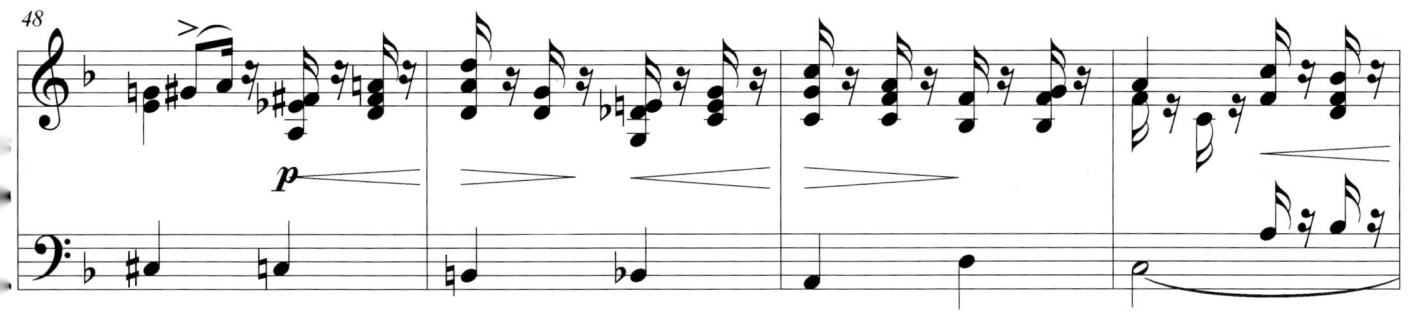
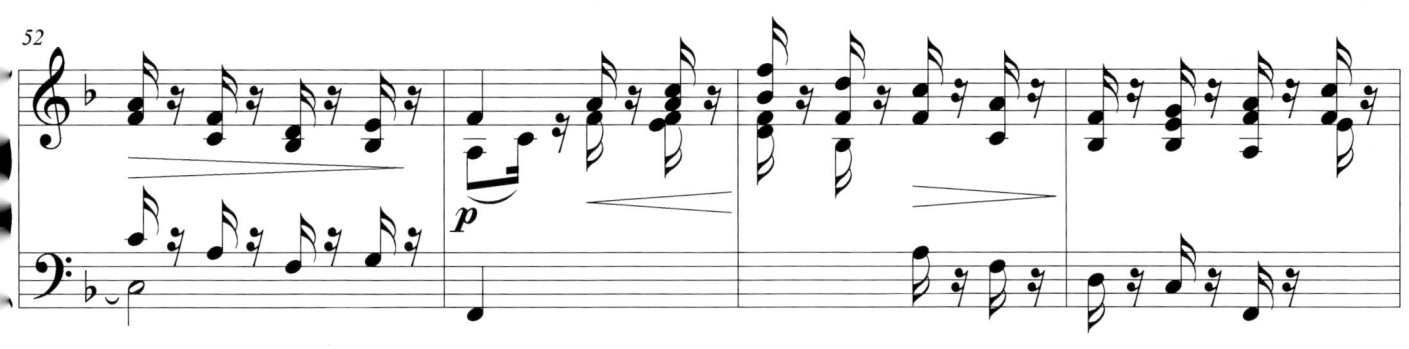

Mazurka, Op. 6, No. 3

Clara Schumann
Op. 6, No. 3

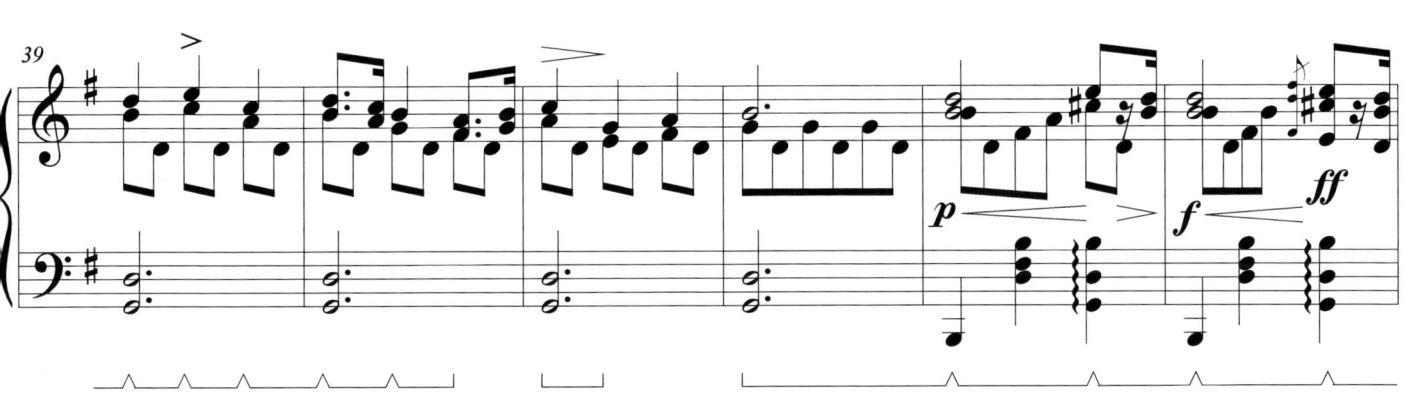

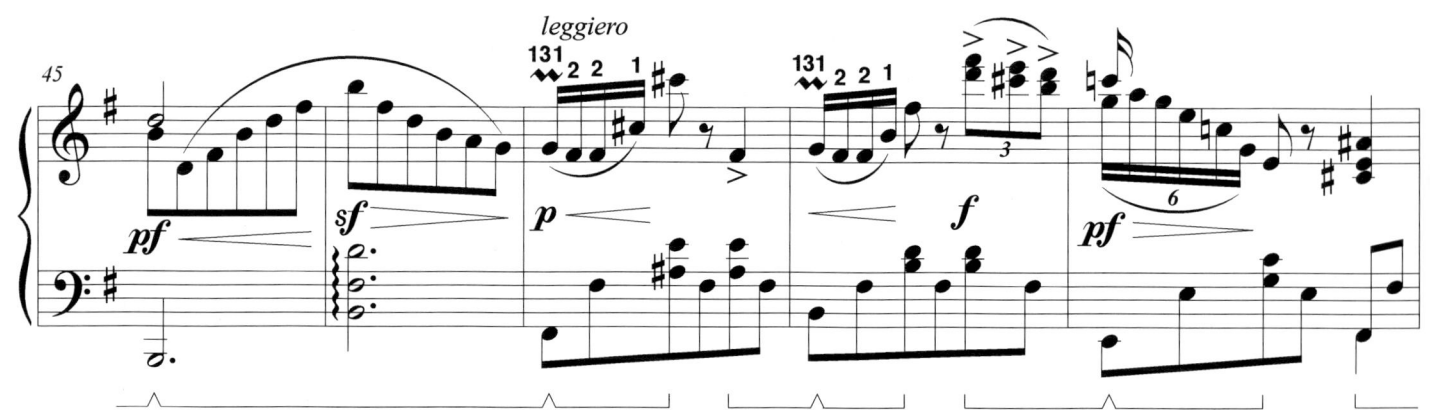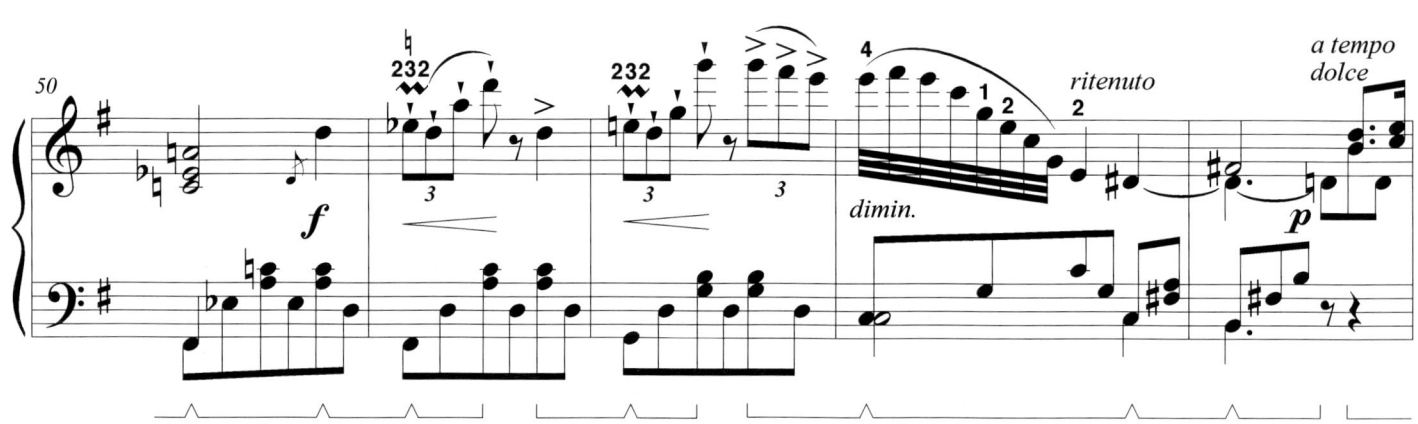

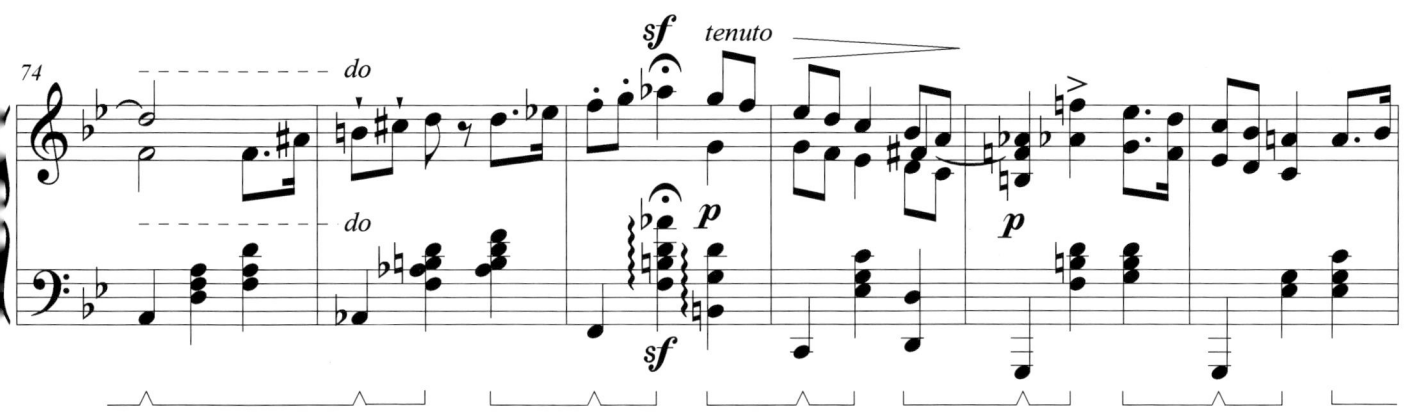
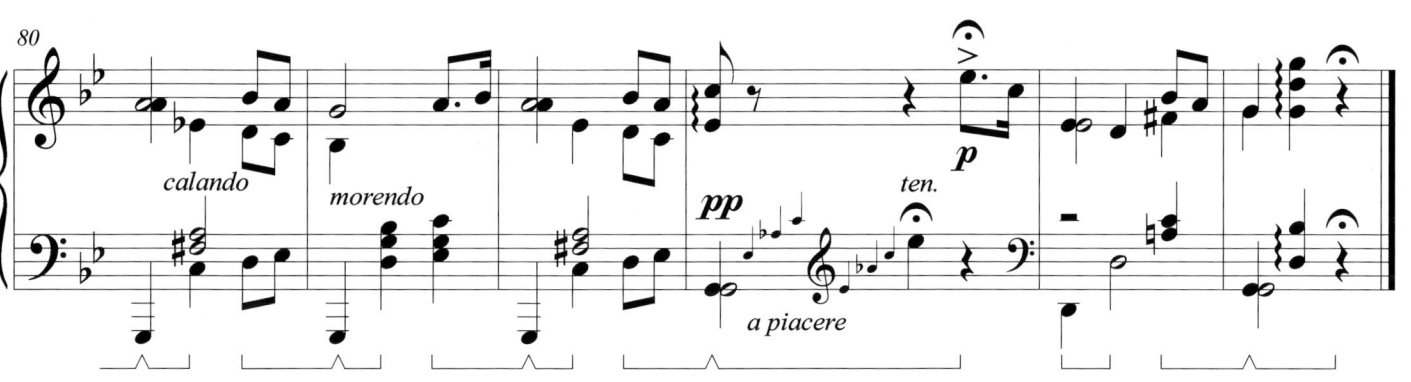

Scherzo, Op. 14

Clara Schumann
Op. 14

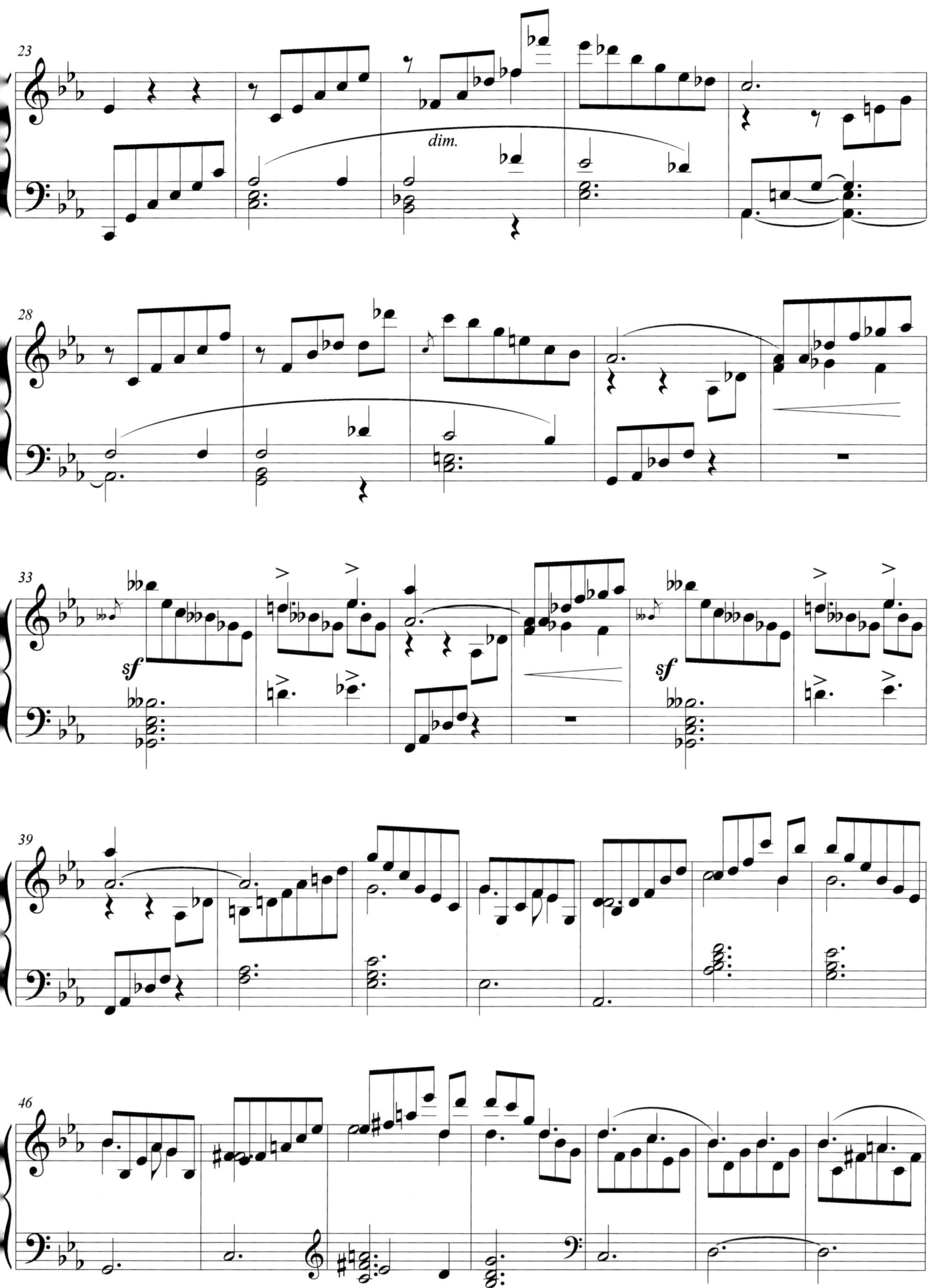

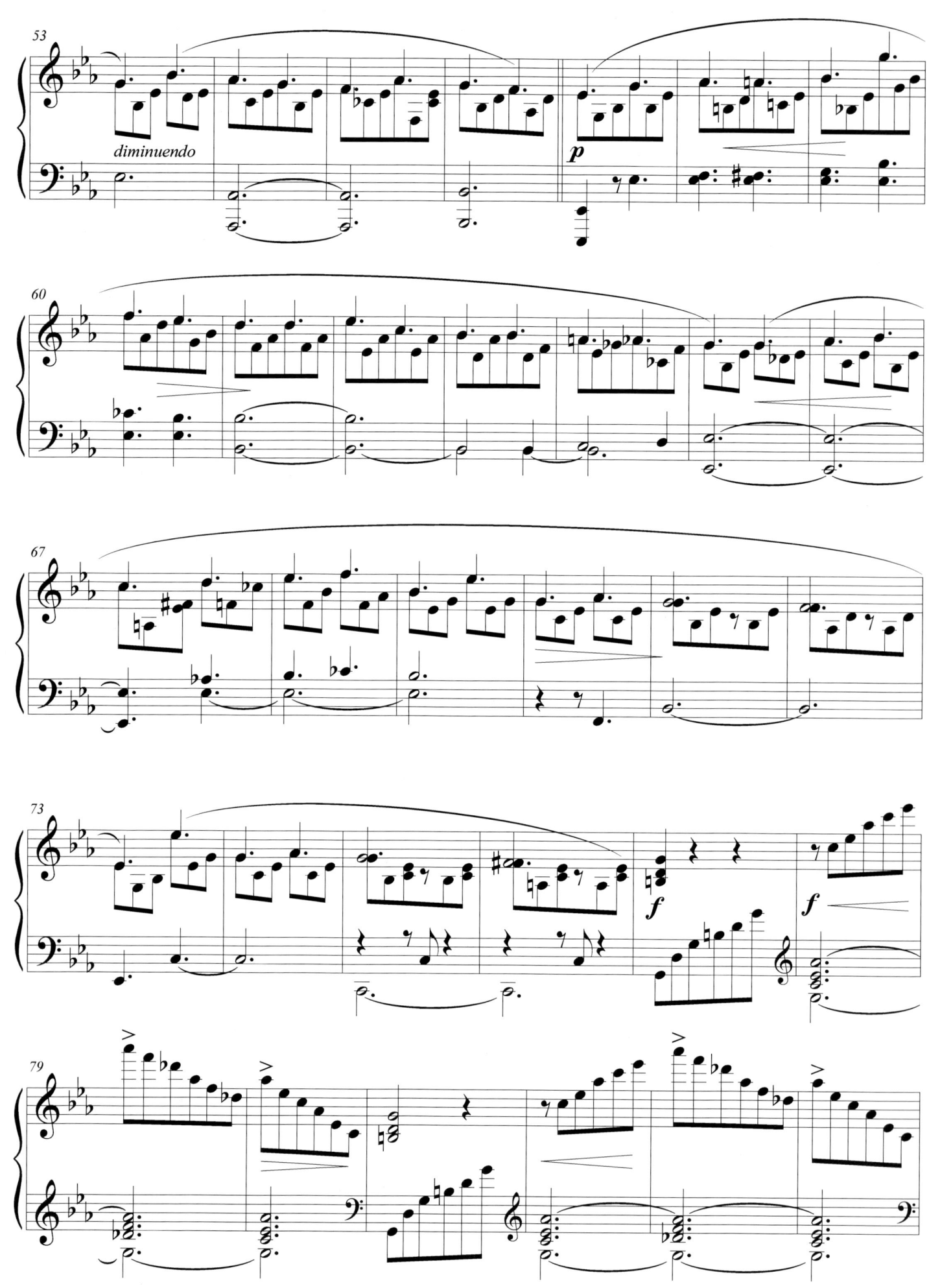

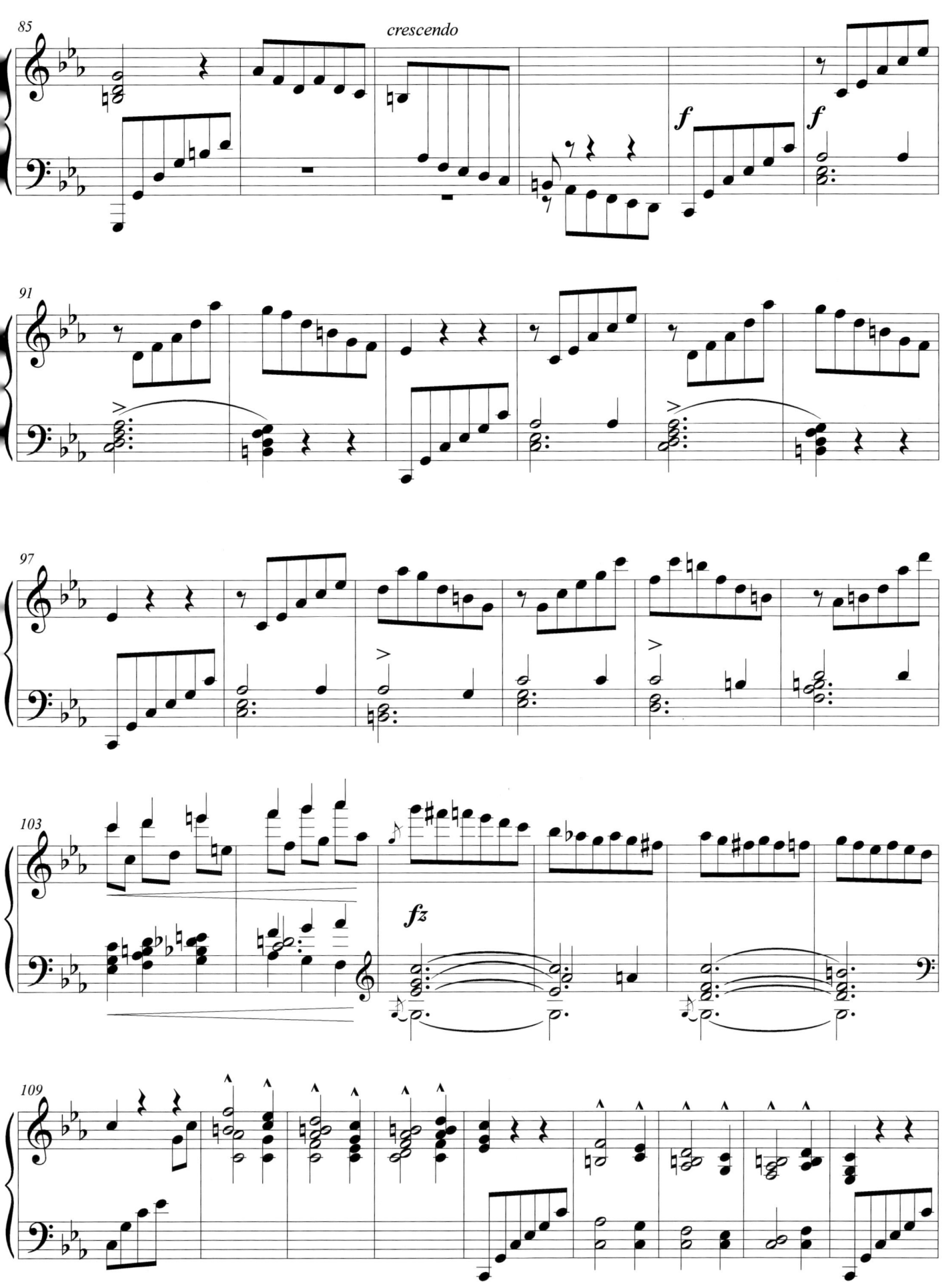

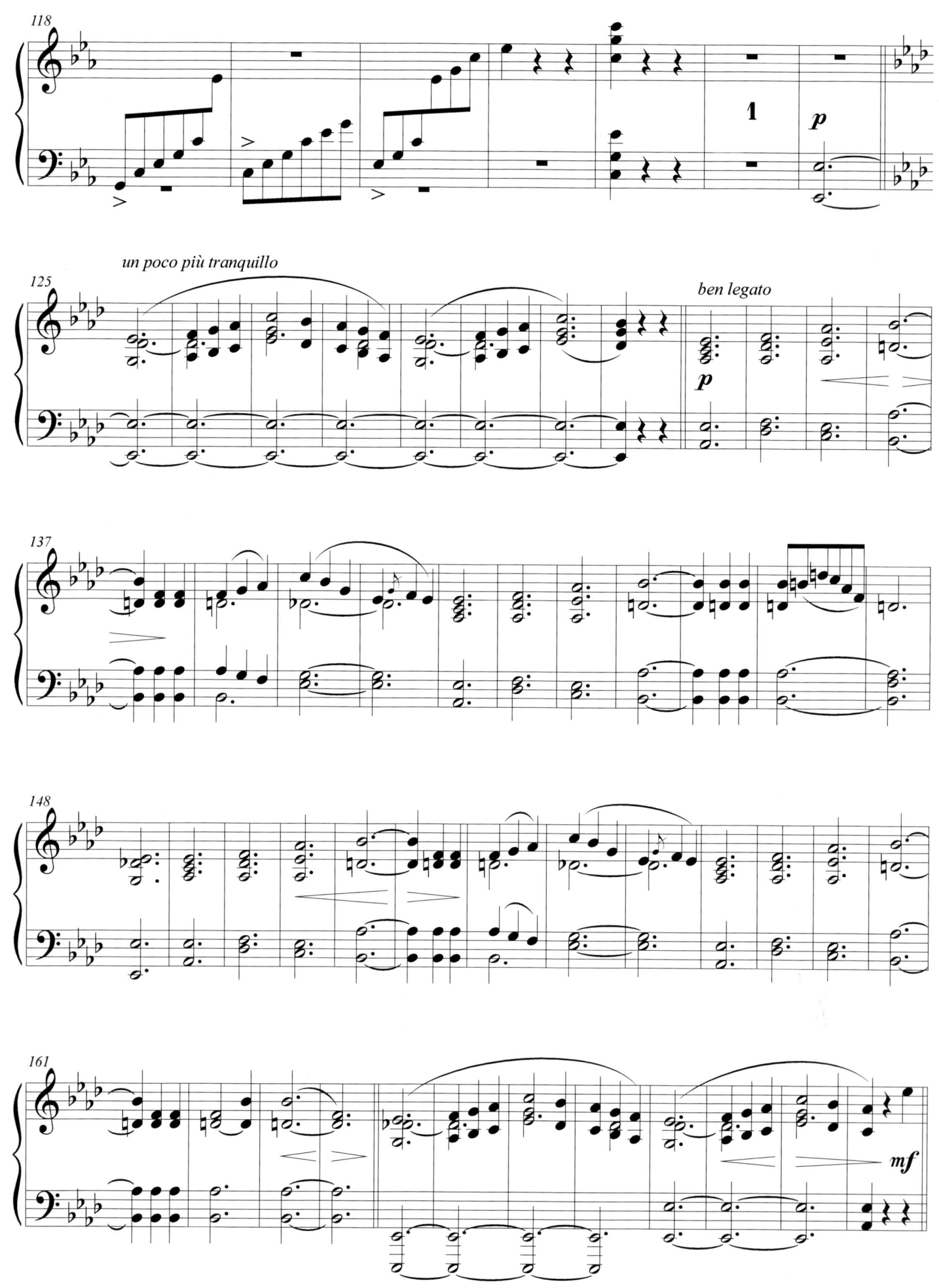

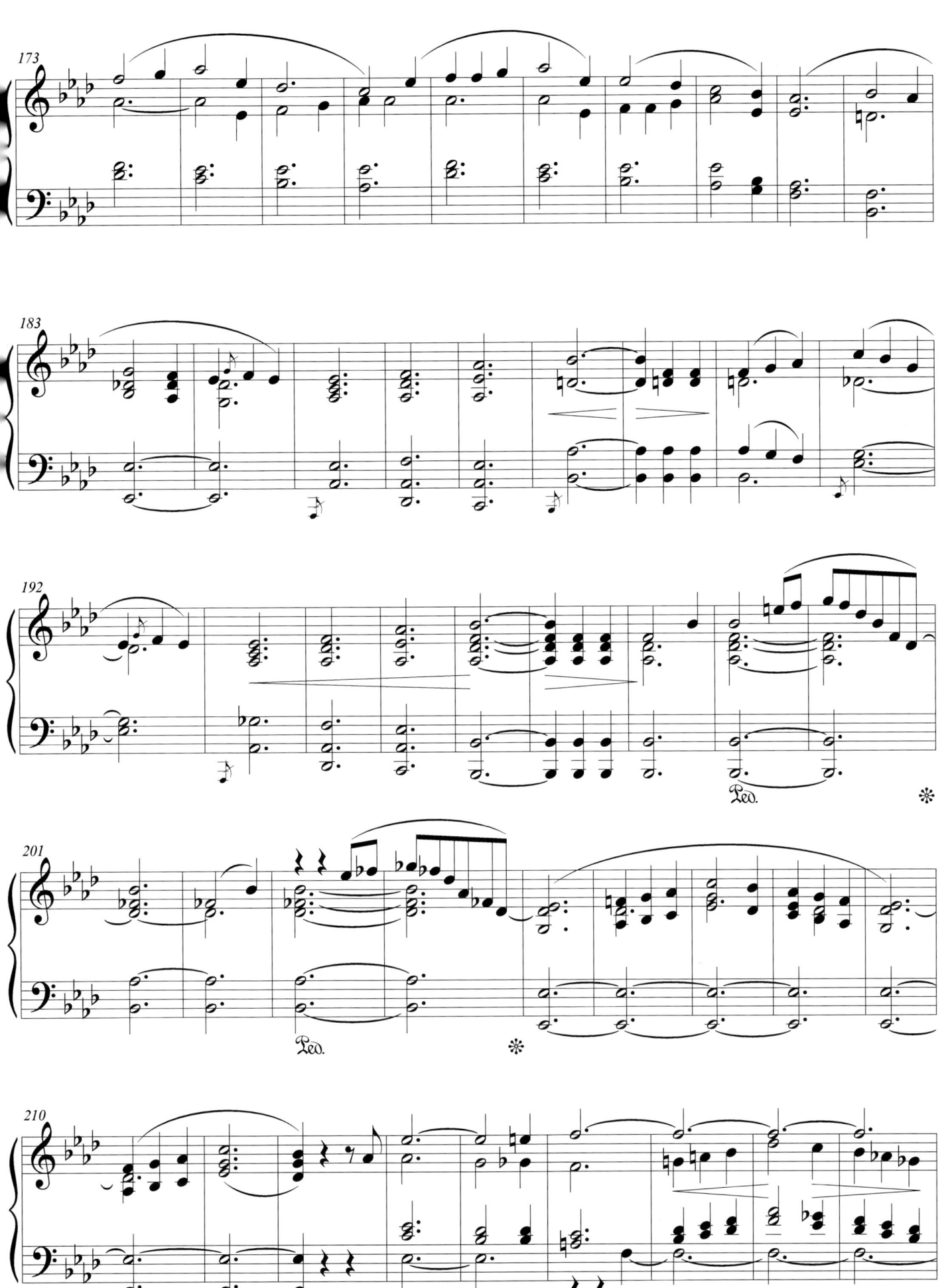

Nocturne, Op. 6, No. 2

Clara Schumann
Op. 6, No. 2

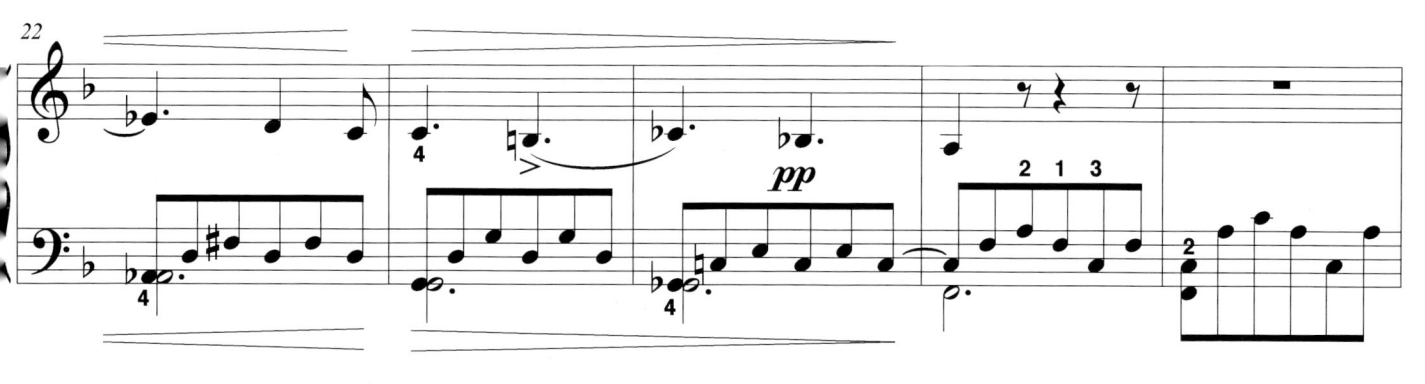
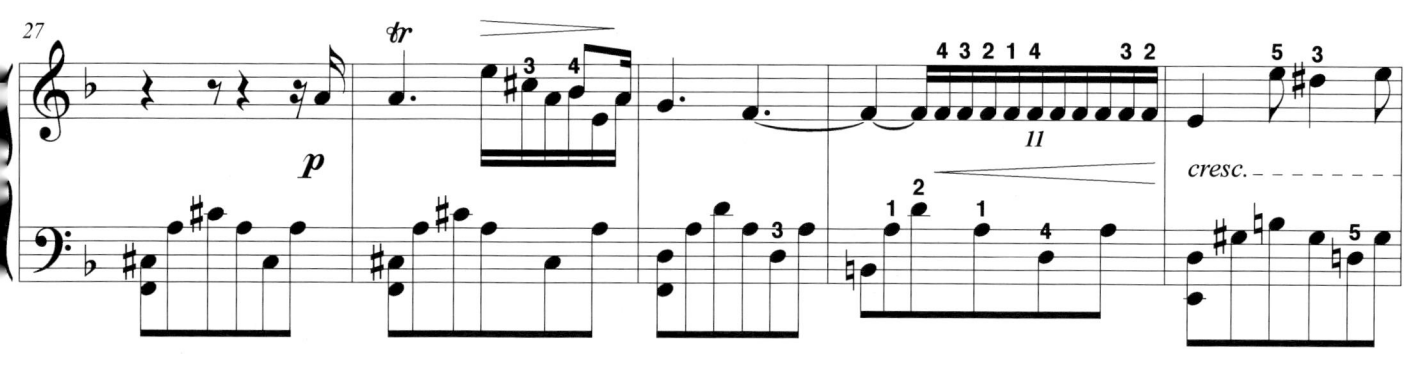
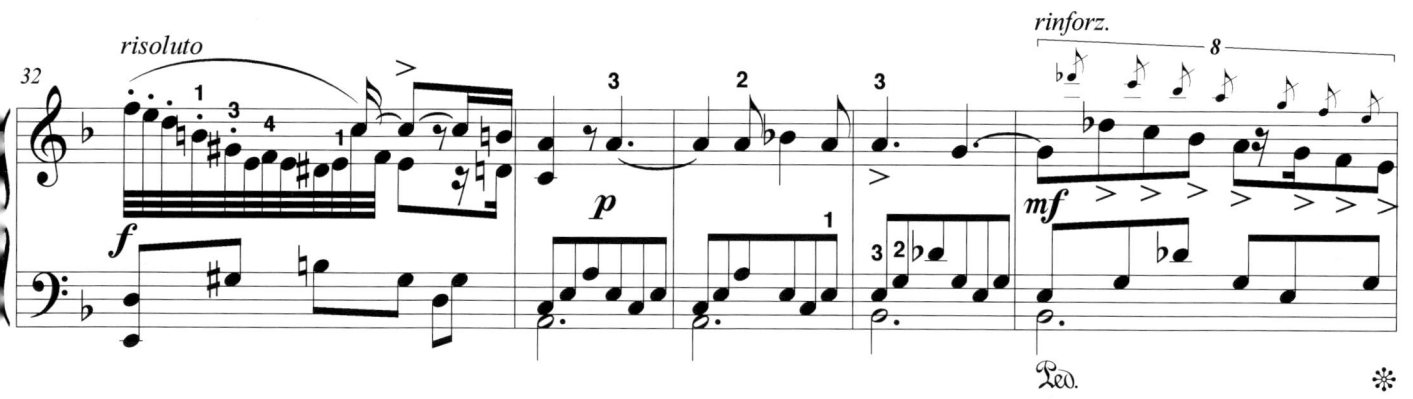
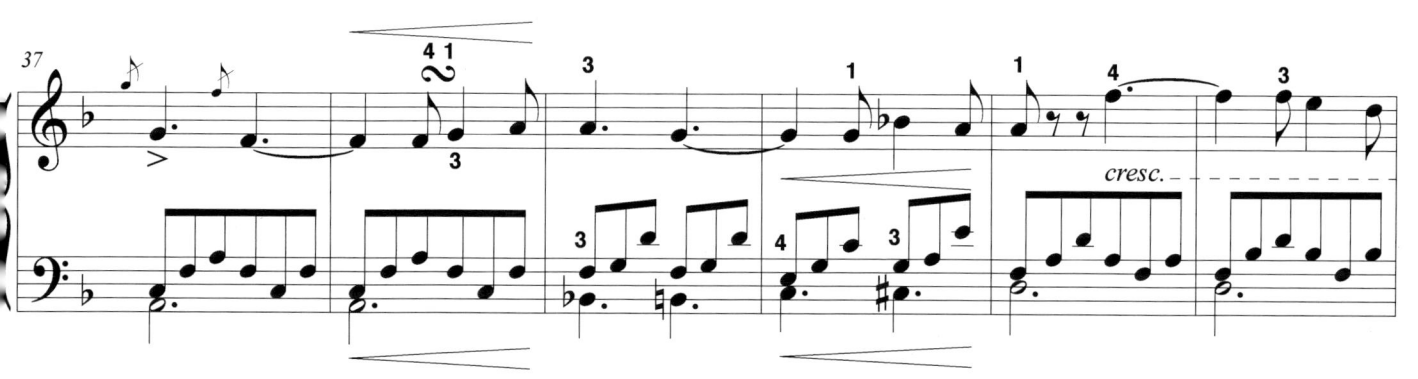

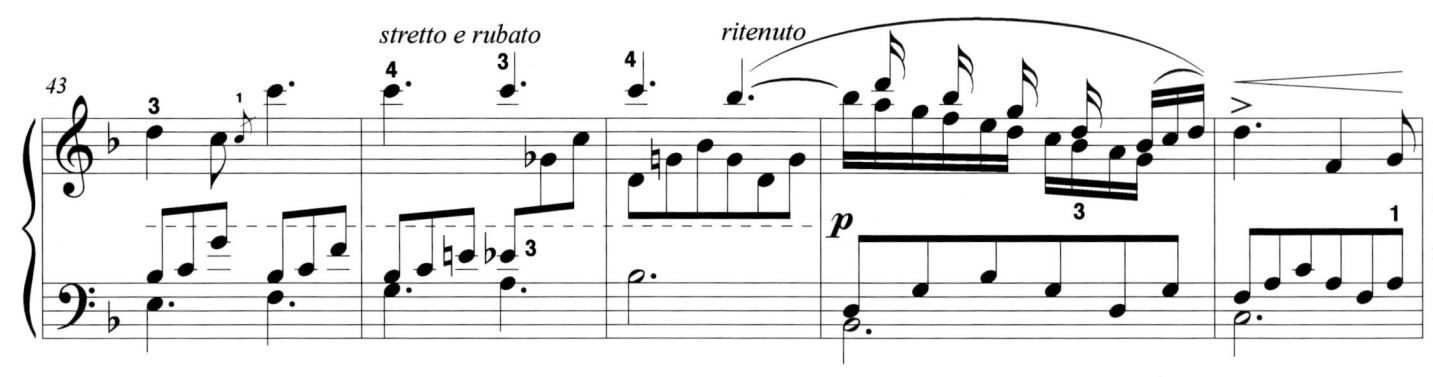

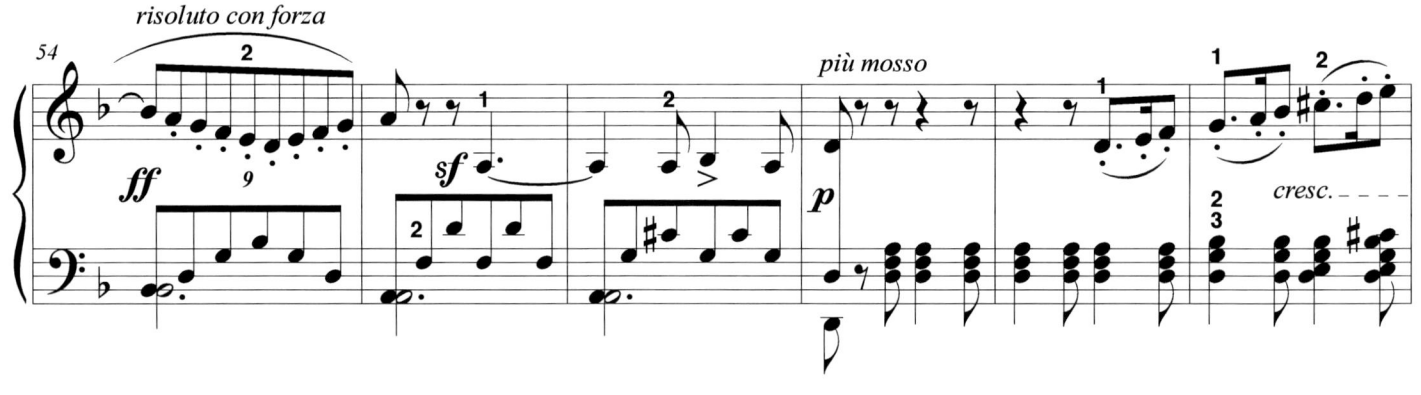
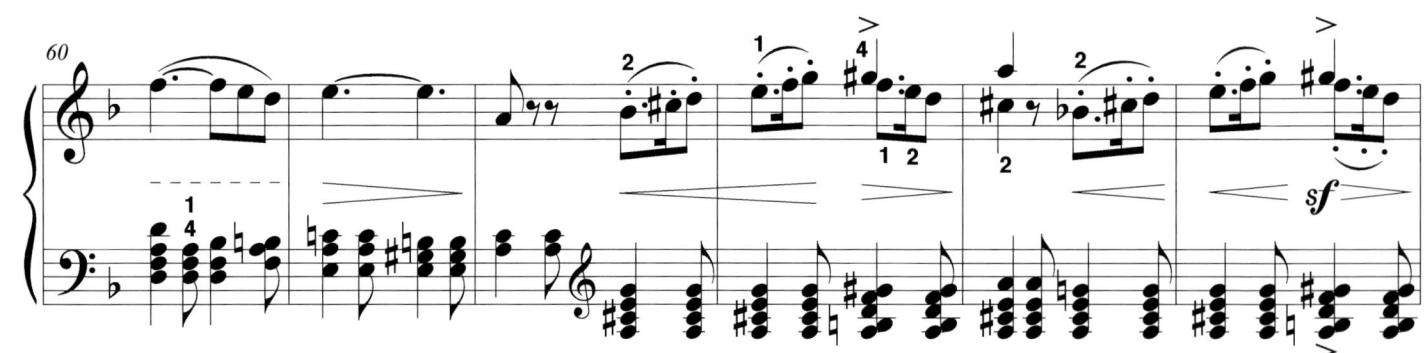

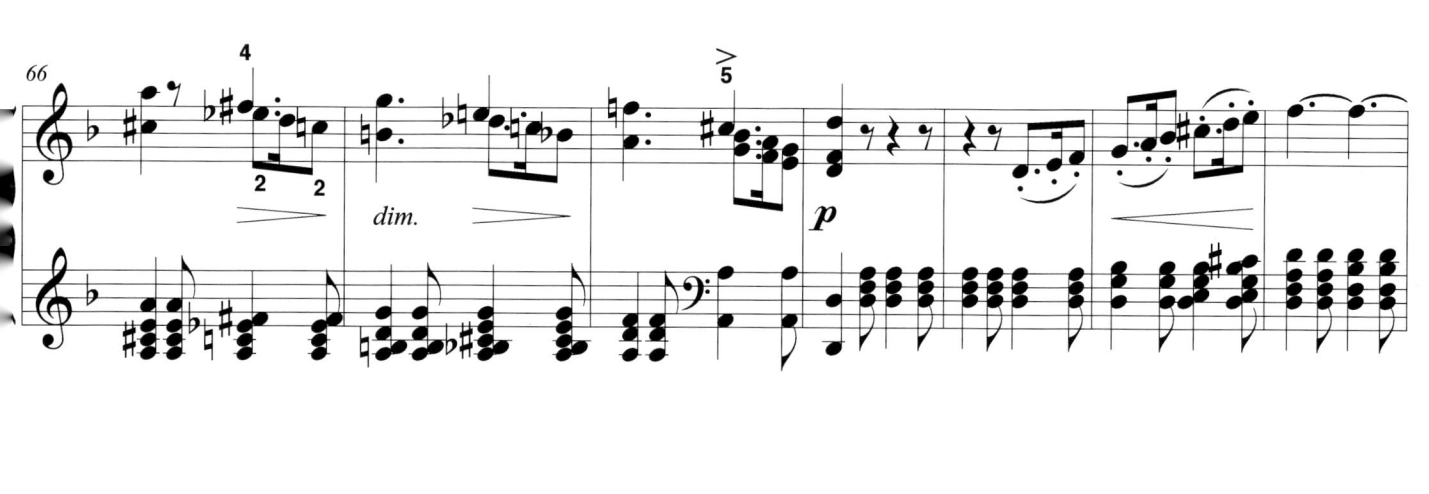

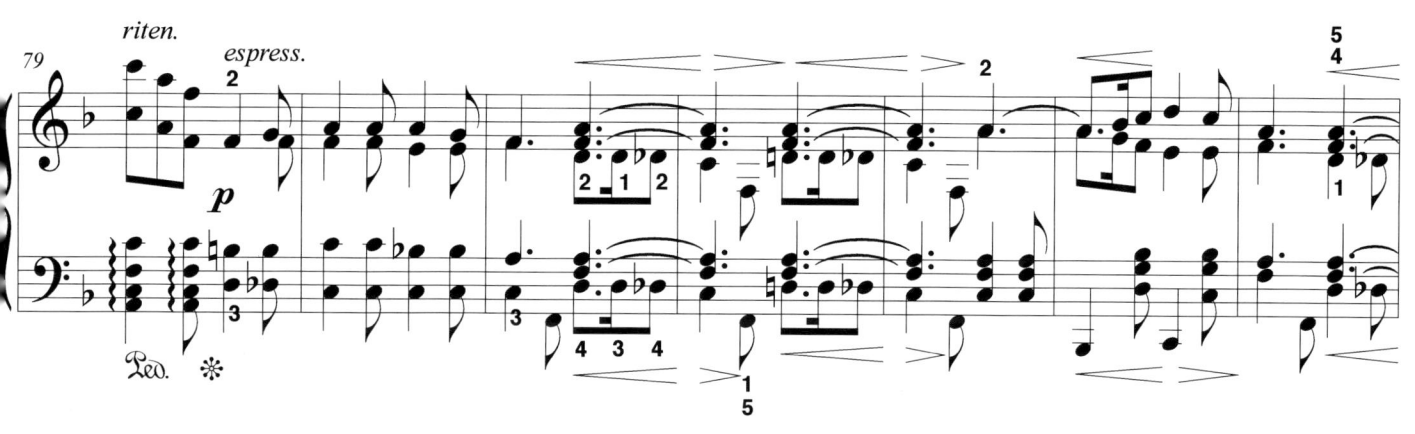

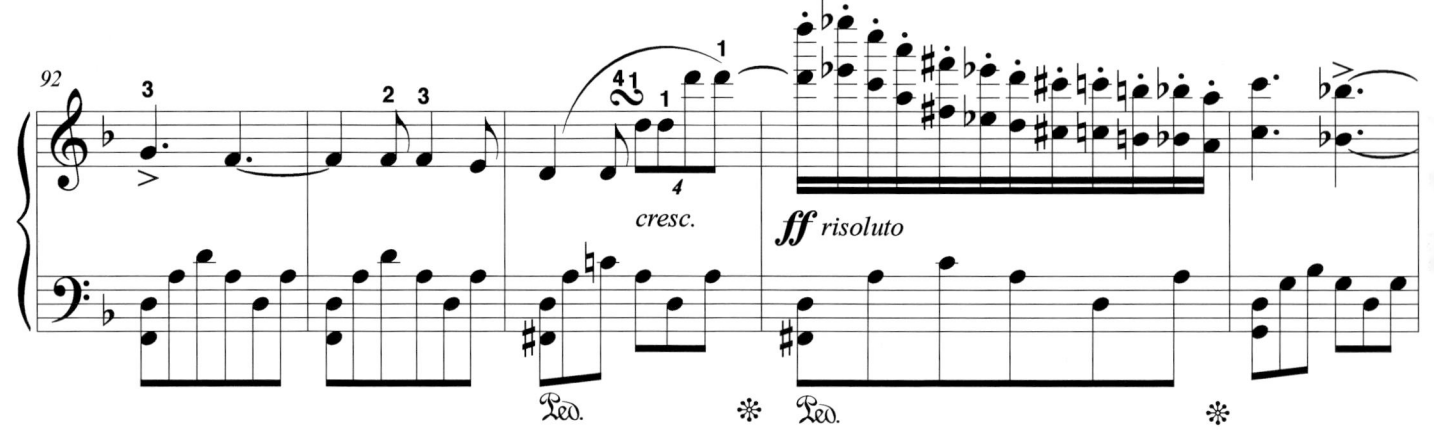
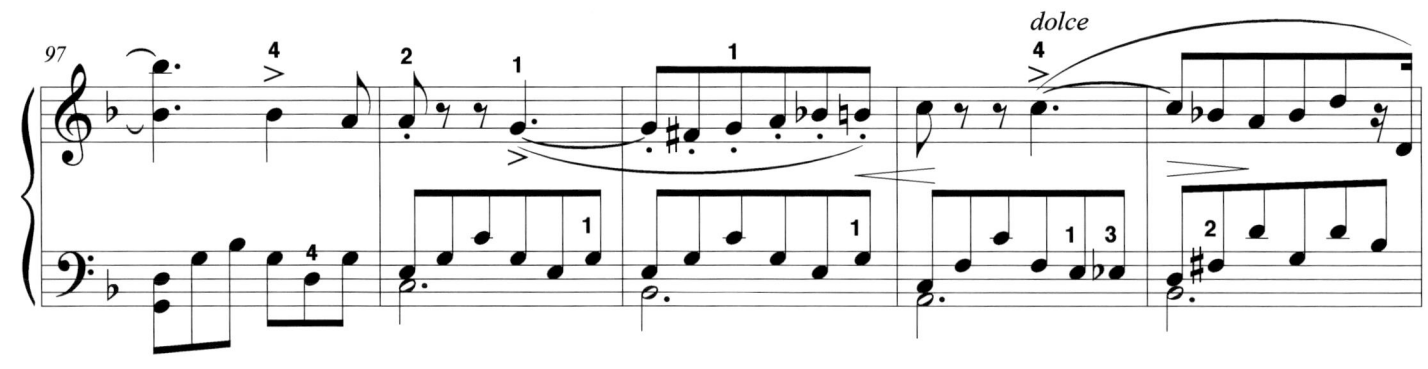
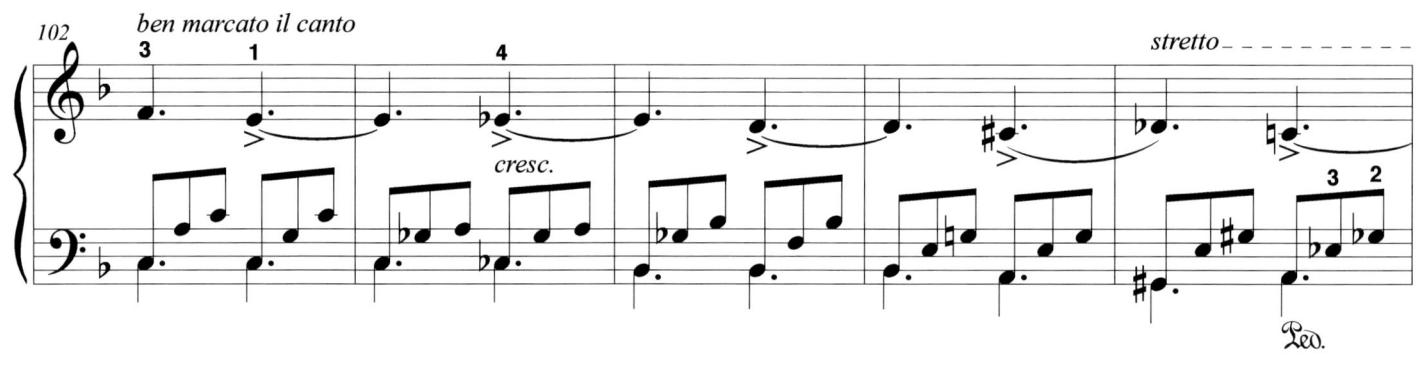
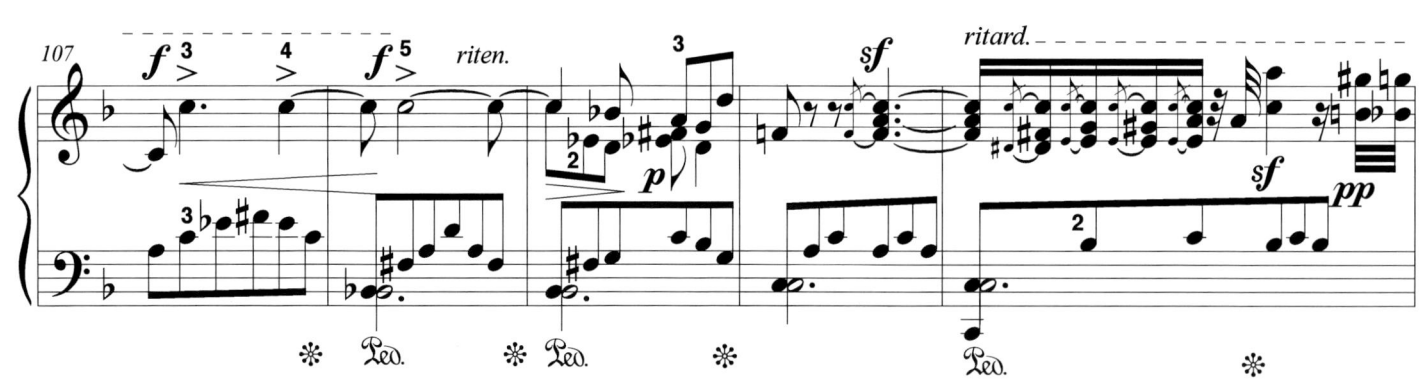

Romance, Op. 3
Introduction

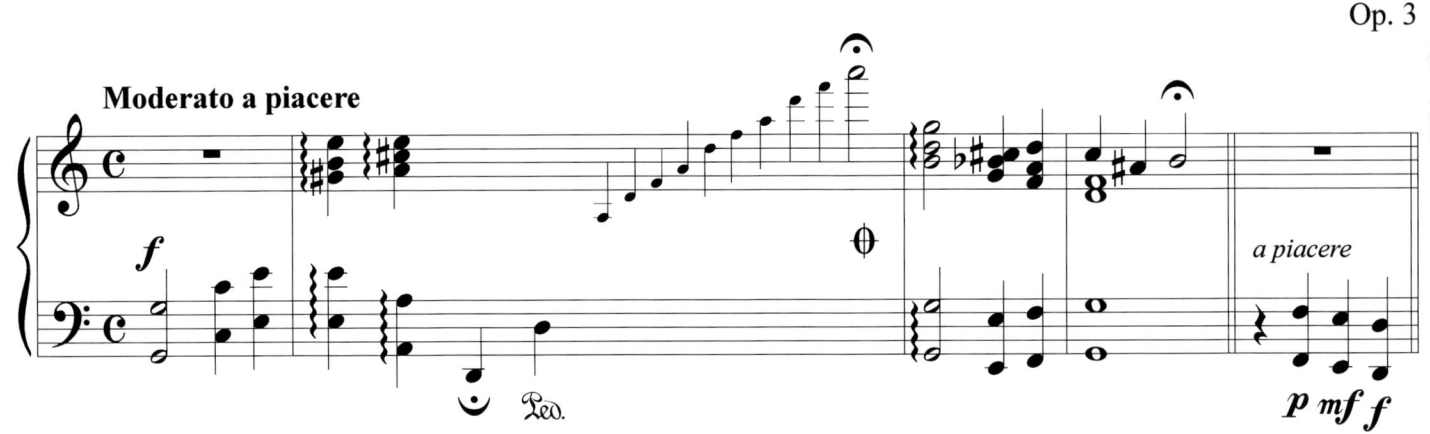

Theme
"Romanza"

Variation 1

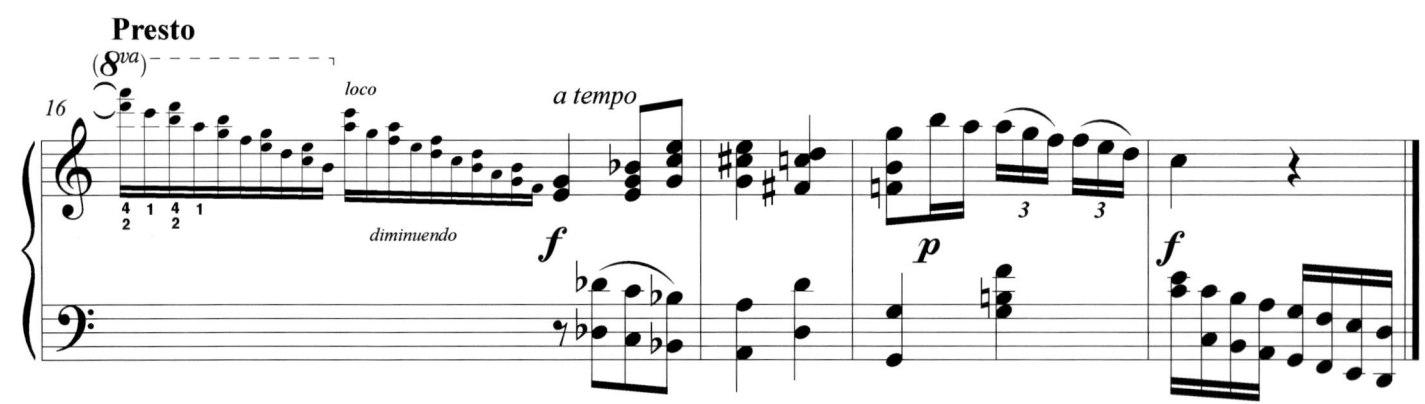

Variation 2

Variation 3

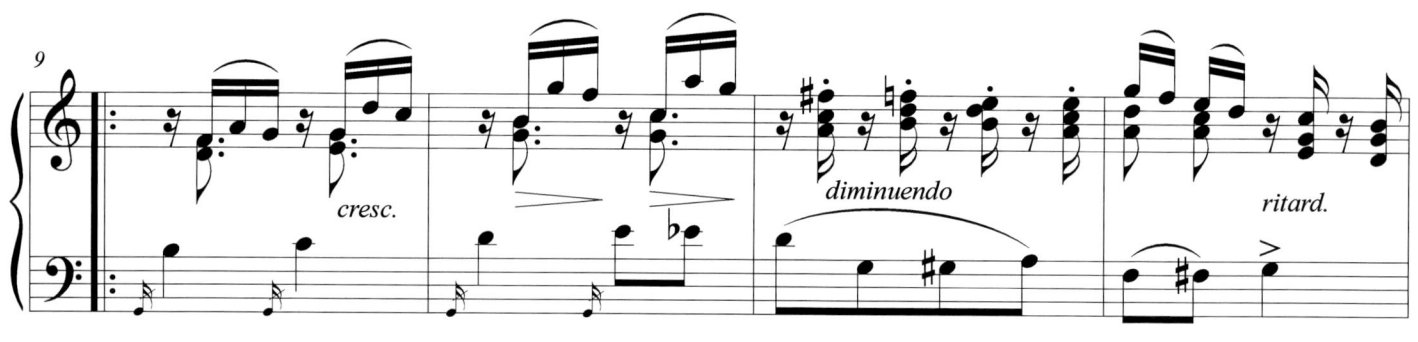

Variation 4

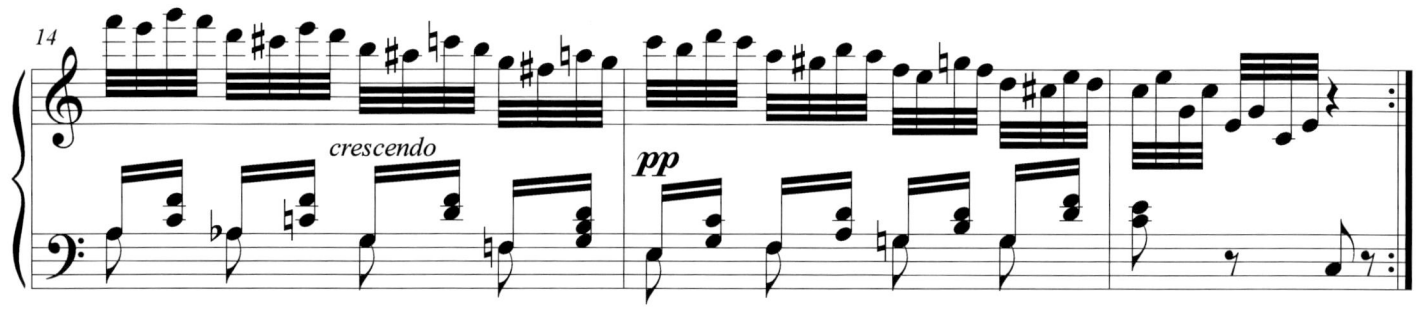

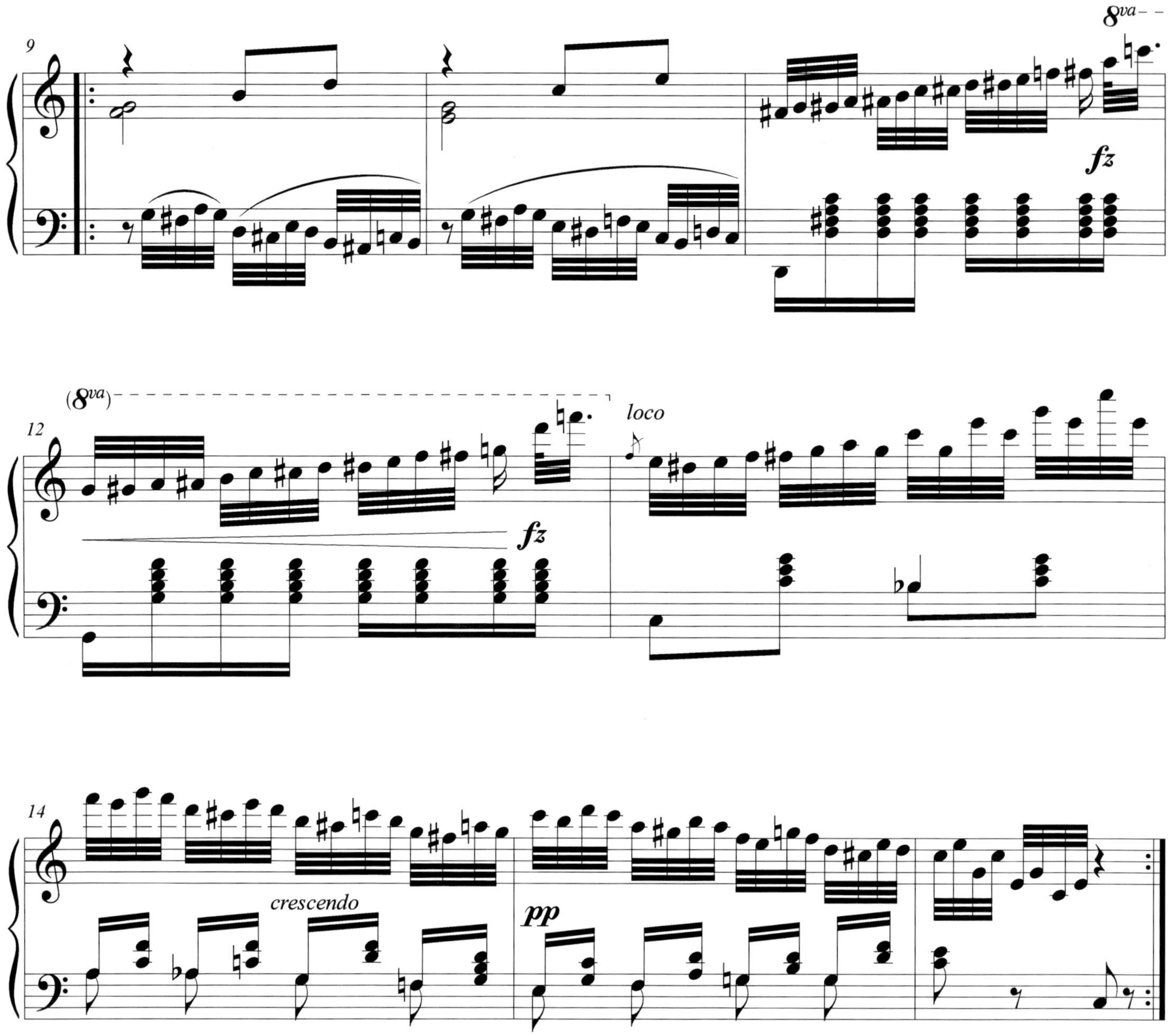
9
8va
fz
(8va)
12
fz
loco
14
crescendo
pp

Variation 5

Variation 6

Variation 7

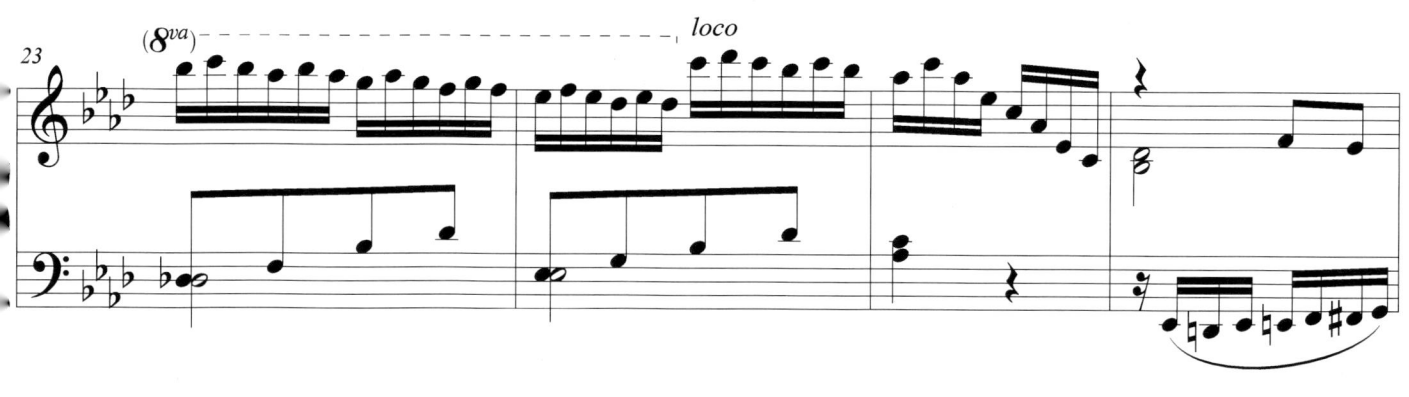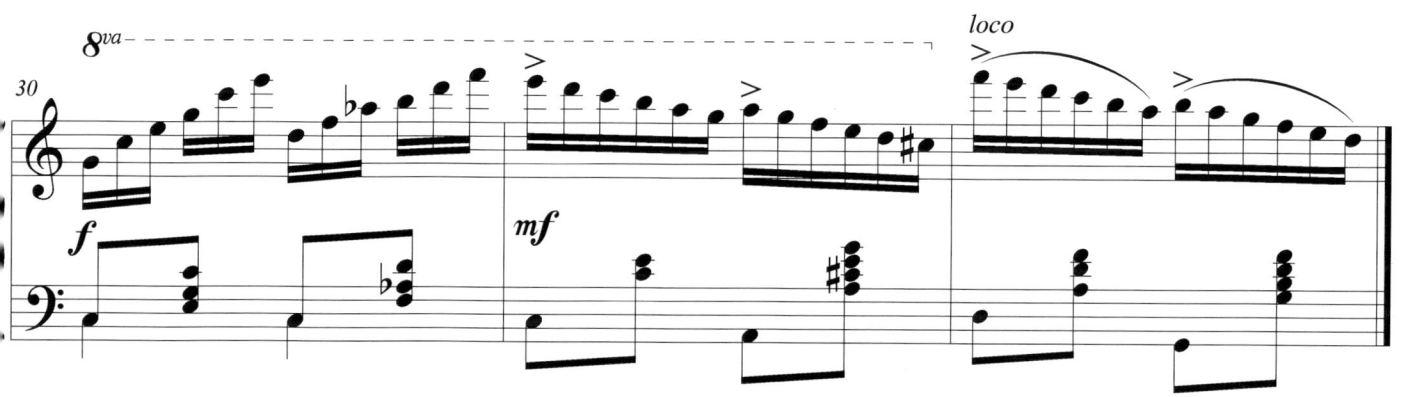

Variation 8

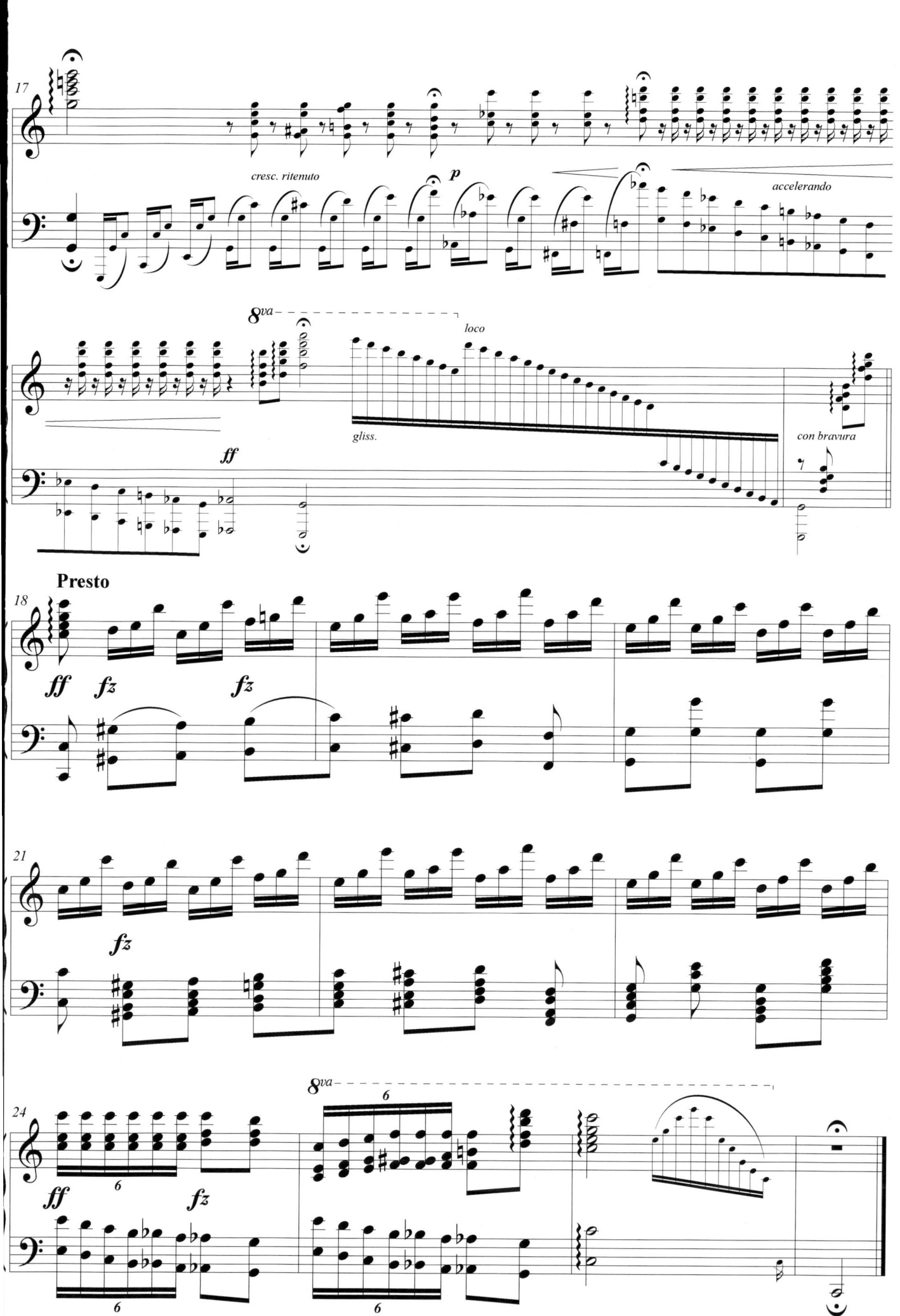

About the Author

Gail Smith received her Bachelor of Fine Arts Degree from Florida Atlantic University. She did graduate studies at Westminster Choir College as well as research at the Mendelssohn Archives in Berlin.

Gail is one of the foremost arranger/composers and is the author of over 50 piano books published by Mel Bay, Hal Leonard, FJH, Lorenz and has a hymn in the Trinity hymnal. Gail is the composer of a unique book of Palindromes that contains pieces that sound the same played backwards or forward and has composed several "Ambigrams" which sound the same upside down, ex. NOON.

Gail was the Music chairman for the Nations League of American Pen Women and president of the local chapter. She has taught students from the age of 3 to 99 and a 4-year-old blind student.

Gail has given workshops on improvisation and concerts all over the U.S. and in Sweden, Germany, and Japan. She has done extensive research on many women composers and is the author of *Four Centuries of Women Composers, The Music of Amy Beach, Women Composers in History* and many others.

Gail gave a concert of Teresa Carreno's music at the Embassy of Venezuela and gave a concert in the historic Trinity Church in Boston where Amy Beach was married to celebrate Beach's 150th birthday. Portraying Clara Schumann in concerts brings every element of Gail's talent into focus.